Mabel and Me:
Who is the glorified rodent?

A mémoire of living cheek by whisker with house rabbits.

By

C A Lewis

Disclaimer

The opinions and views contained in this book are the author's alone. The book is not intended as a rabbit care or husbandry guide as published by veterinary specialists.

CONTENTS

Mabel And Me: Who Is The Glorified Rodent?

PREFACE

So many times, when I explained what it was like sharing my life 24/7 with a rabbit, I saw looks of utter surprise and delight pass across the listeners' faces, often followed with a slight frown of incredulity and the inevitable question 'Is she housetrained?'! Well of course she was, but my naughty side wanted to say, 'No of course not, I just wade around the mess in wellingtons'.

The lack of understanding of rabbits, their complexity, delicacy, nature and 'world view', remains the greatest threat to their wellbeing; it was actually my sister who referred to my first rabbit as 'just a glorified rodent[1]' and I am sure many pet rat owners would be shouting at this page right now disputing the word 'just' in that sentence too!

Other books exist that explore the depth and variety of bunny characteristics, biology, husbandry, some more anthropomorphised than others. This is a mémoire of a period of my life blessed with house bunnies; it is not a manual on keeping rabbits and no doubt will have its

---

[1] Rabbits, contrary to popular belief are not rodents. They fall into another family of animals known as **lagomorphs** of which there are two existing families: hares and rabbits and another called pikas.

critics. Instead, what I hope, is that it is a multi-layered offering, allowing different readers different things to take away, be it humour, problem solving, bonding with a bunny, or help parenting a bunny i.e. being a good human bunny mum. I was fortunate in having the time to spend with them and in solving problems and this book is my chance to share insights and lessons learned.

Regardless, what I hope you will find here is a true joyful observational account of two bunnies' behaviour, focussing on my second bunny Mabel, how I interpreted her actions where I could, or leave it to the reader to decide what this incredible creature was trying to communicate to me as her adopted mum.

INTRODUCTION

After many years of moving around for work, living in rented accommodation and so on, in 2002 I finally reached 'steady state' in life. As such my thoughts began to turn once again to the idea of having a pet. Owning a dog was out of the question as not only would it be left alone all day, but I was starting to suffer some of the long-term effects of an as yet un-diagnosed genetic connective tissue disorder, which would make walking the dog initially difficult and eventually impossible.

Alternatively, I'm afraid I realised I could not live with a cat. Although they seem to like me and it is unpopular to say so, they are causing significant decimation of garden bird life across the country; I would be distraught to find feathered carcasses on the living room carpet when I got home. My opinion was probably partly due to the fact that my sister would happily walk around her cats' latest meal remnants on her living-room carpet; most horrifyingly for me that was often the entrails and bobtails of baby bunnies. I suspect that was a deliberate determination to upset me, as she once left a cookbook open on the table for me to find, showing photos of how to skin rabbits. I am also concerned at the parasite that cats carry and the effect on human behaviour[2].

---

[2] Toxoplasma Gondii
https://www.independent.co.uk/news/science/professor-joanne-webster-the-scientist-who-uncovered-fatal-feline-attraction-8102715.html

I had memories of having a pet rabbit as a child, but my parents were ill-advised, and we were sold two male rabbits. I doubt they were neutered and with their maturing sexuality, they fought through their adjoining chicken-wire wall, causing each other serious injuries. Their unsuitable living conditions, ill-judged companionship and uneducated handling on our part resulted in their ever-increasing aggression towards us children in the form of biting; I suspect it was sheer frustration and I can hardly blame them. It was a very long time ago back in the early 1970s and I am one hundred percent sure it was our collective human ignorance about rabbit keeping that ended in disaster (and probably the cooking pot) for the poor bunnies Benjamin and Peter. Sadly, I will never know their fate.

So I had wondered about getting a rabbit again and assuming it was likely to be only a little more interactive and dependent than a hamster (of which I had had many as a child) I started to consider it as an option. One day whilst in a pet centre, my procrastination finally drove my then boyfriend to say 'Just do it'. I had been cooing over a delightful bunny - a gorgeous lop-eared brown rabbit who came and greeted me as I stood at the side of its pen[3].

---

[3] I would never ever buy a rabbit from a pet shop again; this just encourages 'breeding' of rabbits which they really don't need help doing, and there are hundreds of animal and rabbit rescues filled with 'pet shop' bought or home bred rabbits that need rehoming. Always seek advice, do your research, check they are a legitimate rescue and get in touch with the Rabbit Welfare Association who have loads of useful information on their website as well as a helpline. https://rabbitwelfare.co.uk

Missy

To cut a long story (and an impulsive buy) short, I ended up taking home Missy. She took a few days to name and 'Missy', I should tell you, was short for Mischief. It became apparent within the first few days that timid though she was, this bundle of fur and ears was a quite different proposition than I had expected. She was into everything, nothing seemed to be off limits for exploration or a tentative chew to see if it could be food. Even the bucket of water standing in readiness to change the water in the fish tank was investigated!

As good a place as any to get a drink!

When I 'bought' her, I was advised to buy a large cage, which she would 'happily' live in, and met the welfare requirements that she could hop 3-4 times along its length and could sit up without bumping her head on the roof. Again, it was my ignorance about rabbit husbandry (and what I had learned as a young child regarding how to house rabbits in hutches) that led me to think this was an acceptable way to keep her; it didn't take very long – actually about a couple of hours – to realise that such confinement was cruel, so all my plans to keep her in the cage went out the window.

Over the years I had with her, the affection she showed towards me, who she regarded as her mum, carer and protector, was astonishing. One simple example was at the vets. She needed her temperature taking (which is done rectally) and her instantaneous reaction to the indignity was to leap – all four feet forward – onto my chest. Several times, during hospitalisation for ill health, the vet asked me to come in to see her as she noticeably 'picked up' when mum was there. Years later Mabel showed a similar reaction to a fear stimulus, which was very touching; when the mains smoke alarm in the hall went off in the middle of the night just to warn me the backup battery was a little bit flat, she came belting into the bedroom up onto the bed to me.

My one regret was that my initial ignorance and impulsiveness (and lack of guidance from the pet centre which I sadly witness to this day) meant I got Missy on her own, thus leaving her alone all day while I was at work. Rabbits are crepuscular in that they are active at either end of the day so generally my being away at work during the day was manageable. However, come what may, rabbits need company; they live in groups and are sociable animals. If I needed to be away overnight, at the weekend or even a slightly longer day in the office the loneliness generally resulted in one of two protests.

The first of these protests is pretty dire from the human perspective and more of a 'dirty protest' than a sign of distress; the first time I witnessed it was when I was staying with my boyfriend so we could attend a 'black tie' event. We left Missy in his room with litter tray, plenty of food and water and toys and didn't return until the early hours of the morning. This change in routine was clearly totally unacceptable behaviour as far as Missy was concerned and just to make sure we fully understood the severity of the crime, she made a thorough job of peeing and pooing all over the duvet on his double bed. We opened the door in a slightly tiddly state, turned on the light, and were greeted by this tiny rabbit sitting on the bed looking at us, surrounded by sheer devastation; I honestly wondered how much poo could come out of one tiny rabbit! Suffice to say the duvet had to be thrown away and we spent the night trying to keep warm under a variety of coats, fleeces and sleeping bags.

This protest was often repeated in the first house I lived in with her, as she had access to a sofa-bed in her room. For some reason, soft surfaces seem to induce this behaviour but thankfully it became easy to outsmart her by careful placement of waterproof coverings and easy to wash fleece throws; I of course soon learned that not coming home when she expected was not acceptable, so for her sake I did my utmost to keep to a routine while I was going to work.

The second of the protests is pretty significant from the rabbit's perspective. If a rabbit is unhappy (left alone too long) or in pain they will sometimes simply stop eating. Unlike the rest of us mammals, rabbits have to eat very regularly to keep their stomach and gut working; if they don't they can very quickly go into a condition called 'gut stasis', which if left untreated immediately, is fatal.

Missy enjoying some fresh pulled grass[4]

We had many health scares with Missy and she seemed to have a permanently up-settable stomach, despite a very careful diet. Personally, having now had

---

[4] Cut grass i.e. lawn mowings should never be fed to any herbivore. To pull grass and feed it immediately is fine but after a few minutes chemical changes in the cut grass can cause terrible gastrointestinal troubles which can be fatal.

or cared for many more rabbits with both lop and 'uppy[5]' ears, I am beginning to think an over delicate tummy is a factor or an unwanted by-product of the selective breeding that has developed the lop-eared appearance; but that's only my anecdotally based opinion.

I soon decided that for Missy's sake I needed to find her a boy bunny to keep her company. After a few false starts and rejections, I eventually found her a very sweet little boy we called Bertie with whom she bonded and they were delightful together. He was quite a skittish little lad, but he was there for her not me, so if she loved him that was good enough for me. He settled in very well and readily adopted the litter tray and life indoors and was an exemplary chap.

Missy and Bertie enjoying some spring greens on the landing!

---

[5] In bunny circles, there is an unofficial descriptor for bunny type; 'Uppy-ears' are as you imagine, the ears are either upright or laid back; 'Lop ears', the ears seemingly cannot be raised upright and only turned forward or back in the lop down position. 'Helicopter ears' as Mabel had, is I assume a result of interbreeding between lop and uppy-eared bunnies in that the ears can be held in any position desired together or independently (up, lopped, face forward, face back, sit at half-mast etc.) and have full rotary and vertical movement.

Sadly, I never really got to know him as I would have liked because in 2007 I made the terrible decision to allow Missy and Bertie to be rehomed. Around this time my physical health was making looking after Missy, and particularly the cleaning up I had to do because of her tummy (washing her[6], the study carpet, litter tray etc. at least daily), increasingly difficult. The amount of stress their care was putting upon me was really highlighted when they went to stay with a friend of mine whilst I was having a hip replacement and the following six weeks recovery time. I missed them dreadfully, but found the absence of the physical demands involved a significant relief. Although it broke my heart to allow them to be rehomed, I was reassured by the rescue involved that Missy would be happy with Bertie and that a loving family were lined up waiting to take them. I sincerely believed I was doing the best thing for them and agreed to allow them to be rehomed with someone, where I thought they would get a lot more attention, at least certainly more than I could give them.

Foolishly I trusted the rescue centre owner to follow through with the rehoming, but she decided (wrongly in my opinion) Missy needed to lose some weight first and unfortunately placed her and Bertie with a foster mum. Inevitably the stress of new surroundings sent Missy into gut stasis over night, but because the foster mum had to get the rescue centre's owner's

---

[6] Washing bunnies is covered later in this book but just to clearly advise to never wet a bunny's fur if at all avoidable; washing is a last resort.

permission to take an animal to the vet, Missy was not taken in time and was allowed to die. My friend spoke to me about it a few days later and didn't know I hadn't been told Missy had died. Some frantic phone calls ensued and thankfully I managed to get Missy's ashes from the pet crematorium; I have them still in a wooden casket, decorated with a carved bunny[7]. Bertie was rehomed and I hope had a lovely life. The issue of Missy was one of several catalysts that prompted my friend to part company with the Rabbit Rescue. She felt (totally wrongly) that it was her fault, I knew it was my fault and we were both very distraught; a lot of tears were shed!

I cannot tell you how angry and upset I was at what had happened. I have never forgiven myself and knowing bunnies as I now do, the thought of Missy feeling betrayed by me in her hour of need, will stay with me for the rest of my life. I swore never again! I didn't have the right to have another animal.

But time does heal, and I started wondering if and how I might be able to make keeping a rabbit (or two!) manageable, albeit with my now various and increasing physical limitations. I had learned so much from Missy, I was adamant I needed a different approach. Spurred on by the support and encouragement of friends, I decided I should indeed try and get another pair of bunnies; my mother especially loved Missy, although she later

---

[7] At the time there was limited choice of casket for bunnies; I have since ordered a silver heart casket for her so she can have the same as Mabel.

confessed she thought she was an ugly rabbit - charming! Sadly, from Missy's perspective the relationship had soured somewhat after my mother smacked her for being persistent about something. Unfortunately, my mother didn't realise that unlike a child, a rabbit doesn't understand such concepts as disobedience, so Missy simply regarded her as a threat and avoided her thence forth; all trust was broken. The next time my mother flickered her fingers in Missy's face to try and get her attention, Missy 'boxed[8]' at my mother's hands who then had the nerve to be offended. I did it back to my mother and she agreed having fingers wiggled in your face is not pleasant. But the damage was done.

So, as I now knew the large financial and time commitment needed, this time round I made sure I was fully prepared and fully able to take care of a bonded pair of bunnies; it took quite a bit of forethought and thinking like a rabbit!

---

[8] Rabbits, like Hares will fight or defend themselves by 'boxing' with their front paws. With sturdy claws at the end of these paws, it can really hurt.

CHAPTER 1 – The Preparation (A Rabbit's Perspective)

My new approach was to build a conservatory and fit it out with non-slip, washable and waterproof flooring, an air conditioning unit for summer and a small electric wall heater for winter[9]. Being on the ground floor would make cleaning and litter tray changing a lot easier and the flooring would be easier to keep clean if a new bunny transpired to be prone to an upset tummy! Being downstairs would mean more company for the buns and having the run of the conservatory, with supervised garden visits, would allow enough space to run around without having to 'bunny proof' the rest of the house.

By bunny proofing I mean protecting the bunny *and* house from damage and it involves careful thought. Whilst on the topic, I may as well detail what I mean. In no particular order, first one has to ensure that all electrical cabling or similar, such as window blind cord, is either inaccessible or contained within a plastic conduit or cable tidying tubing. It seems to be a well-known fact that rabbits chew wires – *very* efficiently – and can easily run past a cable seemingly disinterested and mum nearly gets electrocuted later because on that way past

---

[9] Bunnies really suffer from heat; the conservatory soon proved too hot so access to the rest of the house had to be organised; they hate draughts, so fans are not appreciated. The best way to cool a bunny is to use a plant mister filled with pure water to 'mist' their ears or provide a frozen bottle of water wrapped in a towel for them to lean against if they want to.

'somebunny' sliced through the cable. I always know bunny damage because the cable is sliced on a diagonal. I'm not sure how they do it but Missy was the same and it's quite dangerous. Many a time I've been vacuuming and holding the apparently intact cable through my hand as I go, only to feel a sharp 'greenstick' type flap of cable insulation which goes through to bare wire. I suspect Mabel might have had a bad shock (despite her insulating furry feet[10]) because she stopped doing it a few years ago. Coincidentally, she then had a frazzled whisker on the right side of her face that always grew rather oddly, but it didn't put her off doing some considerable damage to the garden hosepipe I foolishly left out on the grass!

The main theory for the cable chewing is that cables resemble roots in the burrow, or twigs with tasty bark to eat. Personally, I think it's all part and parcel of the rubber fetish they seem to have, so second on the bunny proofing list is protection of any items with a rubbery texture. Mobile and household telephone buttons, TV remote controls with rubberised buttons, will all be seen as a yummy treat. Similarly, any rubber doormats or rubber door seals on double glazed patio doors, are all just irresistible. I thought I had damaged

---

[10] Rabbits have furry feet to protect these all-important escape mechanisms from cold, wet, heat, pressure, grazes etc. While claws and furry feet are a great survival bonus in nature, on our human made hard or smooth floors, they offer no grip. A rabbit can break or dislocate legs if startled into trying to run away on such a hard, slippery surface. A recent supposedly funny YouTube film showing a rabbit doing just that did the rounds for a while, but it grieved me immensely.

the Dyson cable and was pretty miffed at its apparent delicacy, until after it was replaced, when I realised what was actually happening.

Missy 'inspecting' the Dyson vacuum.

Third is the importance of making sure there is no access to indoor houseplants as, almost without exception, these will be toxic. Rabbits are excellent scavengers, and will investigate any potential food or drink left accessible; bottles, glasses, cups, anything will get knocked over and investigated. Sometimes just for the sheer devilment of it, a bunny will cheerfully run past something on the floor and give it a nudge, then run away. It took me a while to realise that Missy had a taste for lager and wine as any opened bottles or wine glasses placed on the floor got knocked over. It was only when she thought I wasn't looking that I caught her lapping up the contents of an upset wine glass.

Missy licking the dribbles from a bottle of port

The fourth thing to think about is floor protection for anywhere that may resemble a burrow, for example a small space beside a chest of drawers, as this is ideal 'digging' territory. Carpets withstand digging to varying degrees, so prevention is the best option. This is easily done by placing a cut to size piece of clear Perspex over the area. The fifth consideration, is also a prevention issue; bunnies seem to find wall corners (i.e. an exposed right angle for example at a doorway) very tasty. I'm not sure if it's the paint or the plaster, but either way it's not good for them and it's certainly not an ideal interior decorating effect. The best way to protect them is by simply placing right angle plastic strip on top; apparently bunnies lose interest in trying to get to something once it has been protected. Unlike a dog or cat, rabbits are opportunists and will generally not try and chew or scratch away protective measures, so the strip can be lightly placed using blue-tack or double-sided sticky tape.

Although I don't have wallpaper in my house I do understand that apparently grabbing a loose piece at the bottom and stripping it up the wall is a fabulous bunny past-time. For those with wallpaper, again protective measures are the easiest way to prevent damage and given most wallpaper paste contains all sorts of chemicals including antifungal treatments, funny as it might be to watch, it cannot be good for the rabbit to be ingesting any of the paper or paste.

The sixth item on the list to think about is furniture. I have yet to fathom the intricacies of what makes something irresistibly chewable. There are lots of toys, including chew blocks, that you can buy for bunnies[11], but neither Missy nor Mabel liked them. Instead it seemed to be far more fun to chew something that was 'anchored' in place, but even then there seemed to be no rules. For example, my fabric divan bed – yummy; pine

---

[11] Yes, most bunnies love toys. Though Missy was a great toy user, Mabel really didn't care for them; just one of the many differences between the two of them which also included the fact that Missy adored broccoli and spring Greens whereas Mabel was a beans and kale girl; Missy loved the vacuum happily following it as I vacuumed, Mabel was petrified despite seeing the machine in use at least once a week. Interestingly she showed no fear of a more lightweight vacuum I now have as a replacement. Missy used to willingly come to me for strokes, Mabel tended to come partway and I'd have to go the rest though this changed as she's got older and she came for cuddles at the top of the bed where I could reach her. Missy ate anything offered, Mabel refused pretty much all veg except kale, beans, cavolo nero, some carrots and fresh herbs. I only found out in the last few months of her life that apparently, she also loved rosemary and lavender!

dining table legs – not interested. Beading on the doors of my new bureau style desk – cordon bleu; legs of the antique chair/oak furniture – cursory test nibble then discounted!

Finally, on the bunny proofing front, most bunnies seem to love digging in and rearranging (with their teeth) any fabrics or paper on the floor (and in my experience, on the bed). Missy had two primary habits in this regard, first as I laid my clothes out on the bed in the morning to get dressed she would have to inspect them, rearrange them, sit on them and have a little scrabble at them.

One jumper was a particular Missy favourite (even while wearing a cone-collar to protect post spay stitches)

I got through reels of fluff removing sticky clothes roller. Similarly, if I was wrapping presents on the floor, or doing paperwork, she would decide to try and 'help her mum'. Wrapping paper would be walked across to have a look at the gift, regardless of how much sticky tape we ended up with on our bottom or whiskers, and work papers would be summarily thrown off the sofa or my lap and 'generally sorted' according to a bunny's unique filing system. Where any clothes or papers were inspected, or indeed any rugs, towels, ironing, stripped bedding investigated, with only a sharp set of teeth and strong little nails[12] to do the job, inevitably these items generally come off worse.

Some of the preparations and downsides may seem more trouble than they're worth. But it's no worse damage or mess than a dog, cat or average child would make, and a rabbit can be safe and happy indoors.

So back to my preparations. As the conservatory was nearing completion, I contacted another local rescue who showed me a bonded neutered pair of darling little bunnies and, after some discussion, we agreed I should try and take them home. In all fairness this new rescue had tried to persuade me to take a single rabbit, but given my concerns on the matter and past experience I was fairly insistent that I adopt two. Over several visits these two seemed well-behaved, quiet and hopefully

---

[12] Nail clipping on indoor rabbits in particular is essential for their wellbeing; proper clippers are required and one has to observe all the usual rules such as not cutting into the 'quick' of the nail.

easy to manage such that when I could take them home I did.

I introduced them to their area (the newly built and fitted out conservatory) with the litter tray lined with newspaper and full of fresh hay, bowl of water (bunnies far prefer a bowl of water than a bottle), places to hide, cardboard tunnels, a small amount of pellet food (muesli style foods cause a lot of waste and weight gain as they allow selective feeding) and a small amount of spring greens. I still had several of Missy's toys which I also put in the conservatory.

However within about an hour, once they adjusted to their environment, I realised I'd made a dreadful mistake. They were young, very energetic inquisitive rabbits, who immediately began chewing the furniture, rushing around, and were generally far too fast for me to try and catch or put back in their large 'cage'. With my increasingly uncooperative sore back, I realised I had bitten off more than I could chew and very reluctantly returned the pair to the rescue, as I suspect the rescue owners expected. The little girl bunny had white, grey and brown markings, rather like marble and I had renamed her Mabel, as I loved it as a bunny name.

Coincidentally, while I was preparing for the two new bunnies, an old work colleague based near Oxford asked me if I was still looking for a bunny. She had been made aware of one in need of a new home. I had obviously explained it was too late as I had agreed to take the two from the local rescue. However once this decision was reversed, I contacted my friend who informed me that the bunny she had told me about was still available. As I understand it, another rehoming attempt in the interim had been unsuccessful; this new bunny was already called Mabel[13]!

I drove to Oxford[14] to visit the rescue and met Mabel. She was unwilling to be picked up by the rescue owner (most bunnies hate being picked up – more of that later), but once caught she was placed in my arms. While we talked about practicalities and my experience looking after rabbits, Mabel started to go to sleep and I just knew she was the girl for me as she was confident that I was the right mum for her. This I discovered was actually quite an honour as, since being given to the rescue, two or three rehoming attempts had been made without success. Fourth time lucky for her, it somehow felt like she was waiting for me.

---

[13] I am sure most animal owners have nicknames for their pets: these were a few of Mabel's and don't ask where on earth they came from! Mabelbabel, Delisharabbit, Lumpster Bunster, Lumpy Bump, Schnoz, Pesky Varmint, Hunny Bunny, Lover-bun, Monster Munchingtons, Fluffy Butt.

[14] Small Paws Animal Rescue. Sadly, they have had to significantly reduce their operations due to finances and personal health issues. However, their experience of how rabbits continue to be treated makes that a hard reality to bear.

Mabel – shortly after arrival looking very settled

Normally the rescue, as in most cases, prefer to do home visits to check suitability and conditions before allowing a bunny to be adopted. However whether it was Mabel's reaction to me, my admission that I'd built a conservatory for her, or my comments about hay seeming to be tastier once (euphemistically) 'sat on' a few times, Mabel's guardians seemed convinced that this was a match made in heaven and Mabel came home there and then to live with me. Their follow-up home visit confirmed their assessment.

**Mabel having a yawn and stretch after some top plum chomping!
Its hard work looking this beautiful!**

**Picture also shows cage (with carpeted ramp for traction) set up
as a rather elaborate litter tray.**

Hopefully I have outlined here most of the preparation and considerations I went through before Mabel arrived and upon her arrival. The following chapters go into more detail on living day to day with a bunny.

Chapter 2 – Settling In (Thinking Like A Rabbit)

As with any relationship it takes time to get to know each other, what we like, what we don't like and so on. One of the most important things I learned with Missy is that if you want to understand a rabbit's view of life, you need to try and put yourself in her furry feet. This is difficult and undoubtedly on many occasions I erroneously attributed human emotions to her.

Basically, although they are sociable and playful, they are above all a prey animal. Millions of years of evolution have made them very alert to danger and predators, and to run away and hide when danger threatens. For example, in August 2018 Mabel went to the vet for her usual second vaccination of the year and was seemingly unusually for her, petrified. It transpired that the locum vet who was male was a keeper of boa constrictors and I wonder if her apparent terror was because she could smell them on him. She was funny the three days following this and any sign that she was likely to go in the pet carrier she would run away and hide under the table. That said she was always more scared of men than women.

From Mabel's perspective she was a small potentially tasty snack to this big towering human. I also firmly believe that rabbits are tamed wild animals and not domesticated like cats and dogs who, in contrast, seek out our company and protection. Under normal circumstances I am sure the average bunny would prefer to have nothing to do with us (and given how we treat and house many millions of them I can't say I blame them) so for any relationship to develop, the essential component was trust.

On a practical level there are some basic rules worth observing, and ways to facilitate settling in, even if they can be relaxed later in the relationship.

While bunnies are social animals they are territorial. They have many ways of communicating but it seems scent marking (chinning[15], peeing or pooing) is very important in the bunny world. In the wild, a warren of rabbits will have a latrine a little way from the main burrow which they all use; this diverts predator attention from the main home but also allows family scents to be shared and reinforced. Our pet rabbits have just the same needs but we humans also need to have a say in where that latrine will be in the house! The easiest way to sort both issues is to bring some of the hay from the bunny's old litter tray (i.e. already a bit dirty) and put it in the new one and place the new tray somewhere accessible but private. Having done this, Mabel immediately adopted her litter tray which I located in the corner of the conservatory. Being quite a large rabbit (20" full stretch nose to tail and 3.45kg) it soon became clear that

---

[15] Chinning is a bunny behaviour related to scent marking for territorial purposes. They have, as I understand it, scent glands along the bottom of their jawbone under their cheeks. These they will rub on objects as a means of identification. It is totally undetectable by the human nose and leaves no residue; I'm not 100% convinced why they bother but it must mean something to a bunny!

your average litter tray wasn't going to meet her needs. After a few trials (and errors) I found the best option to be an under-bed storage box minus its lid, some 40cm by 58cm, and 18cm deep.

The 'litter tray'

I knew she was in there somewhere!

The cheapest, healthiest and safest contents for the litter tray are a newspaper lining topped with a mix of straw (the stalk residue from cereal farming) and hay (dried grass) in a roughly 1:3 ratio. Quality of hay especially can vary considerably; the only way you can really check that it's fresh and not in any way musty or mouldy is to conduct the 'sniff' test. Basically, if it smells fresh and good enough to eat then buy it, if it smells musty or damp reject it; the quality of the hay (freshness and level of dust extraction) will have a major impact on a bunny tummy and bunny breathing. This latter issue is the reason one should always reject shredded paper (too dusty), cat litter (scented and/or potentially edible) or wood shavings (totally unnatural for a bunny and often strong smelling[16]) as absorbent media. Mabel's litter tray, being quite large, allowed her to sit and go to the loo while chomping away happily on some hay or straw – a favourite pastime for nearly all bunnies I've known. Generally I gave her a clean litter tray every other day with the daily top up of hay at the very minimum.

The second thing I did with Mabel, which I think helped her settle in, was I initially left her with minimal noise and interaction. I allowed her to expand her area of familiarity gradually over several days, one room at

---

[16] The same applied to cleaning products and anything strong smelling. Bunnies have delicate little noses so even perfume can be overpowering to them. The same goes for their delicate little ears and excessive noise.

a time which reduced the feeling of panic; if the route back to safety or 'home' isn't clear or remembered it can cause a lot of stress. She quickly explored the sofa and cushions in the conservatory and clearly enjoyed playing in amongst them. It's the only time I ever saw her truly burrow. The pictures tell the story and she had me in stitches; I so wish I'd had a phone with video back then.

**Mabel having fun on the sofa – on three different occasions when
I had camera to hand.**

Thirdly, to try and build trust, I avoided picking her up. As she expanded her territory, I allowed her to come and investigate me. Sitting on the floor with her and armed with treats such as a dandelion leaf[17], I allowed her to interact with me on her own terms but with a little bribery to help matters along. From my experience with Missy I knew the trust would only develop over time and as long as it was never betrayed. Hitting a rabbit for example as my mother did, is not only pointless as they don't understand cause-and-effect, but will also immediately mean you are categorised as a potential predator and not to be trusted.......EVER!

If I did need to catch her to take her to the vet for example, I put a procedure in place which she could learn to understand and hopefully feel less threatened by. Keeping the house quiet and calm, I gently herded her into a single area such as the conservatory where there was minimal furniture and hiding places, then with a pet carrier ready, tried to gently herd her into it. If this failed, a slow persistent walk following her around the room got the message across in a nonthreatening way and let her know that I meant business.

If I needed to physically pick her up I had a similar strategy of gently following, but repeatedly gently saying 'pick up' so I think she recognised what I needed to do and she would let me know she was ready to be picked up by

---

[17] There are different types of Dandelion leaf I discovered; Mabel would only eat one type.

hunkering down[18] close to the floor, letting me stroke the top of her head and remaining still while I picked her up. This routine avoided a battle and avoided inducing her fight or flight reactions, either of which could be injurious to both parties! Making her feel secure in this process also helped and it was critical to ensure she had one firm hand under her chest and one under her bottom supporting the back legs; leaving legs to dangle as would be tolerated by a cat or dog is a massive 'no no' for bunnies.

Countless rabbits are injured by struggling free from being held badly, falling to the ground and backs and legs getting broken. Feeling secure and being held quite snugly seemed to make her feel calmer about it all and far less likely to struggle. I shudder at the thought of any rabbit being picked up by its ears as magicians of old used to pull the rabbit out of a top hat. Their ears are not handles; we do this to no other animal, so why assume it won't hurt a rabbit? I don't know of any cat or dog owner who would even dream of picking up their pet by its tail or ears. I think I would kick up a bit of a stink if someone tried picking me up by my ears!

Anyway, I'm unsure how I did it or started doing it but both Mabel and Missy accepted once picked up, being held like a baby in my left arm with their head in the crook of my arm, their back along my forearm and bottom held securely in the palm of my hand.

---

[18] Hunkering down is the best way I can describe the way Mabel would tuck her feet in under herself and sit very solidly on the floor ready to be picked up.

Lying along my arm, hand under her bottom, drying off with an old tea towel.
(subtext: 'really mother?')

This shouldn't be confused with something called trancing where a rabbit is laid on its back and apparently seems to go completely passive. This is sometimes used as a means of treating rabbits by some vets and owners, however it's a sign of abject terror and actually a last-ditch attempt by the rabbit to get away from a perceived life-and-death situation. Basically pretend you're dead and your captor might drop its guard long enough for you to come to life to run away or maybe seem less of an attractive meal if you are already dead.

Above all I tried to set a routine of where and when she would be fed, where she would sleep etc. as bunnies really take comfort in routine. Something new such as new furniture can be fascinating, but a new or very erratic bedtime can be stressful. Change in routine can cause significant behavioural issues as will be discussed later, though my house move from a four-bedroom house to a two-bedroom bungalow went surprisingly well, especially as I had to live in a Bed & Breakfast with her for some time while the bungalow was being renovated.

That said, probably the change that could cause the most trouble is the introduction of a partner rabbit. Whenever possible a neutered male and female is the best combination for a bonded pair, even better if they are littermates. I deeply regretted getting Missy on her own without her sister (also a good combination but less ideal) at the pet centre back in 2002. If a male and female are to live together neutering is essential. Not only does it stop unwanted litters of rabbits (a 2010 study by the Rabbit Welfare Association conservatively estimate some 67,000 unwanted rabbits are surrendered to rescue centres every year across the country[19]) but it also has significant health and behavioural benefits. Female rabbits are very prone to cancers in the reproductive organs (though poor Mabel developed a tumour on her uterine stump; whether this was just bad luck or inexperienced surgery prior to my having her, I don't know), and both male and female rabbits are far less aggressive, likely to fight or likely to scent mark (spray urine) if neutered.

Having adopted Mabel on her own, I really felt I should try and find her a partner. I knew she had had three failed rehoming attempts which I assumed involved

[19] 'Rabbits in rescue – it's worse than we thought'. RabbitingOn The Magazine for Rabbit Lovers. Spring 2013 Hastings Printing Company.

a failed bonding, but I felt I couldn't promote bu
pairing yet have a single rabbit myself.

Bonding rabbits a is complex process and I
personally think you either have the knack for it or you
don't and my bunny friend had succeeded with many
a rabbit bonding. Most notably she bonded two males
and one female rabbit as a group of three although one
of the males was disabled and the other exceptionally
good-natured this was still highly skilled and best not
undertaken by most bunny parents. If you don't have a
bunny friend with the magic touch, really it's best carried
out (in my opinion) by bunny experts such as a well-
respected rabbit rescue owner. With enough experience
they will soon tell from an initial meeting whether the
signs are positive and a bond likely to form.

After the initial 'meeting' (assuming all goes well)
the real hard work starts. The rabbits need to be kept in
adjacent areas, and their litter trays swapped daily so they
become used to each other's scent. After a few weeks,
its then time to swap the bunnies themselves between
the two areas. Over time, hopefully they will be regularly
sitting beside each other, either side of the wire of their
enclosures. This is all best done on neutral territory.
Eventually after some chaperoned meetings, if all is well,
they will settle down together. There may be a bit of
squabbling as one rabbit claims the dominant position,
but assuming the other is willing to submit, generally they
will be ok. Thankfully being such social animals, on first/
second/third meeting, generally they will only display
disinterest in the other if the bond hasn't worked.

I tried twice to find Mabel a bonded partner. Both times resulted in abject failure! First, was Henry, a very beautiful blue grey bunny with 'uppy' ears. The first meeting at the rescue was positive, and I went through their bonding process in my garage (neutral territory).

Mabel & Henry in the back garden

All went well, for a few days, and they got up to quite a bit of mischief together. Their worst crime was only discovered one morning when I couldn't find them....... anywhere. I then noticed that the footrest of the powered recliner sofa was up enough that, I assume Henry being the more lithe animal, had got underneath, and once inside knocked out the protective Perspex barriers at either end of the sofa allowing Mabel in and both were nicely ensconced under the sofa. My then boyfriend was not really bunny savvy and having asked him to always ensure the footrest was down at night after use, on this occasion had forgotten. Unsurprisingly, they had done a lot of damage; seemingly almost expertly, they had chewed the cables coming out of the power adaptors to the motors, literally a couple of centimetres from the boxes! Whilst chewing this end of the circuit probably saved them (and my house) from going up in smoke, it meant repairs were shall we say tricky?

After a few weeks, it seemed Mabel was determined to be boss and one day all hell broke loose and they fought bitterly. I was not prepared to take the risk of ever leaving them together on their own which totally defeated the object so Henry, sadly, went back to the rescue. I think he was probably an ok little chap, I suspect it was my feisty girl who was the problem. This suspicion was rather supported by my next attempt.

I was contacted by a pet shop with whom I had left my contact details to say they had just had a rabbit brought in for rehoming, would I like to see if he would be suitable for Mabel? I went to see him, and totally fell in love. He was a sweetie that was obvious; he was in a fairly tiny cage and I just thought, come what may, I have to try and help him. I was afraid of naming him in case it all ended in disaster, so I just referred to him as (the) Little Man and it stuck.

Little Man with Mabel

This time I didn't trust myself to do the bonding and my friend agreed to take them both into her care so they could be bonded on truly neutral territory (and without me!). She didn't let me down and after a few weeks they had bonded and returned home to me. All was well, there was the odd scrap but nothing serious, until I think I made a massive mistake. As will be expanded on in the next chapter, Mabel loved sleeping on my bed. As it was a king size I had one side with a single duvet, and she had the other side which was protected with waterproof covers just in case, and topped with easily washed fleece throws. I suspect she liked the elevated position and being next to me, her adopted mum (and associated cuddles and treats), and from a dominance and safety perspective. Anyway, at night she would come up on the bed while Little Man was left alone in the hall. Feeling sorry for him, I encouraged him to come up on the bed with us and picked him up and placed him next to us.

This was a step too far for Mabel and she jumped off the bed in a huff. The next day relations between them were strained if not frosty, and later that day they had a dreadful falling out. I intervened and was accidentally bitten, but it was a price worth paying to avoid injuries to them and frankly I deserved it for being so stupid. I doubt they would have done much damage to each other at that stage, but I couldn't bear to see either of them hurt.

After this, I gave up. I realised that whilst I was thinking 'I'm being selfish not finding her a bunny partner, she should have a bunny chum', she was probably thinking 'you are my bunny chum despite lack of fur and silly little ears; why do you keep trying to introduce someone new – and a *boy* at that!'. Gross anthropomorphising I know but I suspect not far from the truth.

But this meant I was left with Little Man needing a new home and I just couldn't bring myself to abandon him at the pet centre, he was such a lovely bunny. Thankfully my friend agreed and bless her heart she took him in. It was Little Man who bonded with a female rabbit and disabled[20] male rabbit. After the female passed away, the two boys were fine together; I think Little Man just wanted a quiet life. When the disabled bunny died, my friend successfully bonded Little Man with another female.

If there is one thing that made me want to recount these stories and highlight how wonderful these animals

---

[20] G had been ill with Encephalitozoon cuniculi which had left him with a bad head tilt; despite this he seemed to enjoy life, have a voracious appetite, and lived to a ripe old age!

are is how Little Man behaved around his disabled friend G. Whilst my friend was away, I was on emergency call out for her rabbits and I needed to take G to the vet. Following best practice, I took both G and Little Man together in a pet carrier in the car. I noticed that however gently I drove, any cornering resulted in G rolling over onto one side or the other or sometimes even ending up on his back due to the effect the Encephalitozoon Cuniculi had had on his balance system. At first I thought Little Man was just being a fidget, but I soon noticed that as G rolled one way, Little Man would move to that side to try and prop him up. Then to the other side as required, back and forth. I can only assume there was not only problem solving going on in that little bunny brain, but also significant empathy or understanding of how G was feeling, as in the end Little Man lay across G to help keep him still, stable and upright.

If an animal behaviourist can come up with an alternative interpretation other than problem solving and empathy then I would be willing to listen, but this action was one of the things that made me so determined to write this book; I just had to get the word out there that these are intelligent, caring, loving and kind animals that deserve so much more than we give them.

Knowing Little Man was happy made it easier to bear losing him and Mabel became ensconced as a very present force of personality in my home. While her introduction to me and my home had been (hopefully from her perspective too) a success, she still had a massive amount to teach me as we muddled along together day by day.

CHAPTER 3 – Day To Day (Living Like A Rabbit)

So back to Mabel and our day to day living. The one thing I can say is that everything took longer with a bunny; I just had to stop and give her a kiss or a head rub every time I went past as she popped her little head out from under the hall seat for attention or in the hope of food. There is nothing softer than bunny fur and a kiss on the top of her head always elicited a chunner[21] of appreciation.

For a good relationship to develop between you and a bunny, you need time as well as that all important patience, persistence and perception. Our routine and my health was such that I spent a great deal of time with Mabel at home. The best way to describe our daily routine is to go through a typical day. Out of respect for her crepuscular body clock, I will start the 'day' at 10PM.

She would sit and wait in the hall for her evening greens and drop unsubtle hints if they weren't forthcoming. She would go into the kitchen where her claws made a noise on the flooring, and sit and wait at the fridge door. At other times she would often beg for a bean while I was getting anything else out of the fridge, which she then ran off with into the hall.

---

[21] A chunner is what I call the quick light grinding of the teeth and noisy breathing, almost huffing. I assumed it was the bunny equivalent of sighing but was not to be confused with proper tooth grinding as that is a sign of something being very wrong.

Around 10PM it was sort of time for bed; if I didn't come to bed at the normal time (I said bunnies love routine) I would be given several hints that it was about time I got myself together. In my last house, she would run upstairs and onto the bed. If I didn't follow, I would hear the thump as she jumped off, and look round to see her peering at me through the banisters from the second to top step. Since moving to a bungalow, she started to do the same (sitting on the bed waiting) then running to and fro from bedroom to living room, nudging my foot as she ran past if I wasn't coming to bed fast enough. If I still failed to do as I was told, I would hear scrabbling on the bedding; I'd long since given up worrying about the bed clothes or fleeces on her side of the bed[22]. All my duvet covers (and sheets for that matter) were full of slices and holes (I later found my pyjama top had been chewed while I was asleep one night: I guess if I had the temerity to turn my back on her what should I expect?).

Having a good dig at mum's duvet.

---

[22] My partner around that time slept in the spare room; his snoring would wake the dead!

Before I started getting ready for bed, she had some/all or a combination of the following on the bed: a large piece of carrot, a large handful of chopped kale, a handful of round beans, watercress, some potted mint, thyme and parsley, and some of her pellet food. The source and freshness of these items was critical. She would only eat Waitrose kale willingly but would eat other brands if pushed (except M&S for some weird reason). After a while she turned her nose up at kale, preferring instead the very expensive 'cavolo nero' or black kale as its also known; I ended up buying 6 packs of this a week and at £1.50 a pop it wasn't cheap. Waitrose was the only place I could get it that was acceptable, though a budget supermarket did start doing it at half the price for a short while.

Chomping some fresh thyme; tricky if it's all tangled up.

I didn't blame her for getting bored with the same thing day in day out so I tried to vary what she had, but she was a fussy eater and like us, she would go through phases of food preference, sometimes preferring kale over cavolo nero or vice versa. Sometimes she preferred one treat over another[23]. Even in her old age when food was in the offing she could hop around circling my feet very enthusiastically; this circling (sometimes accompanied by honking or grunting) is a misplaced mating behaviour which has been adapted to mean – 'I love you (human) mum, please can I have a sweetie?'

I found that she preferred to have the cavolo nero leaves 'de-spined' so she could eat them in one long piece; I rather likened it to having to remove the crusts off a piece of bread for a fussy child. I also quickly learned that bowls were pretty useless, as most would get tipped up; can't blame her really, if it was easier.

Bowls just got tipped up.

[23] Be careful about treat quality and check what you are feeding your rabbit; I found nylon string in one very well know brand's treat bar which could have killed her had she eaten it assuming it was hay. Little notice was taken by the supplier, manufacturer or vendor; I guess rabbits don't matter.

Once, in an emergency to get her eating after a period of bad health I bought her organic carrots so she could have the tops; my plan to eat the carrots myself fell through, as she soon rejected the ordinary carrots I bought her in preference for the organic. If a bunny can tell the difference, there has to be something in it!

I put night lights in the living room and hall for her, so she could see her way to her litter tray. The one time I forgot to turn them on, she stood on the end of my side of the bed looking into the dark hall till I got up and put the nightlight on. She then jumped down and ran off into the living room to use her litter tray. To ensure she could see coming up and down off the bed, I burnt an eight hour nightlight in an enclosed lantern; just enough for her to see where she was going without keeping me awake. It only occurred to me after having to replace the switches when the touch switch broke, that I could have put a dimmer switch in!

Different bunnies have different foibles and one of Mabel's was chewing fabric. The living-room curtains were lifted off the floor with tie-backs, but there was little I could do about the bedding. Although I did notice one thing that initially I couldn't understand was that the bottom of my clothes (trousers), towels, sheets etc. were getting shredded. I quickly realised she was adopting the clothes airer in the kitchen as a burrow and the clothes were getting 'arranged' into suitable positions with her teeth. The airer was relegated to the loft and other drying methods employed!

Back to bedtime, once she had her fill of greens she would hop over to mum and snuggle down for a good body and head massage. Her appreciation was shown in two main ways. First was 'chunnering', and the second only started in 2015 when my friend and I came back from a holiday and it involved serious grooming of my hand and arm. She was looked after by a very competent pet sitter[24] but obviously didn't get her usual cuddles which may have focused her mind. The only time I've ever had my face licked was January 2020. In fact at night time later in life, she would rest her chin on the dividing wall of cardboard I had in the middle of the bed to keep her on her side where the fleeces and waterproofing was. It was very sweet and plaintive as she was definitely looking for love and affection.

Somewhere to rest our little head whilst awaiting affection.

---

[24] Holiday care is a serious consideration and additional expense you have to factor in. Depending on the bunny, its single or bonded status, where it lives (outside pen or indoors) holiday cover can be an issue. Even if housed in an outdoor pen, the holiday care provider needs to be rabbit savvy, confident picking rabbits up and knowledgeable about signs or symptoms that need intervention. In general, as rabbits dislike change and are prey animals, boarding them at a cattery or kennels would be extremely stressful.

Bunny tongues are really quite hot and quite smooth, and she could get into almost a frenzy of grooming where she started trying to groom my 'fur' with her teeth. I am sure I don't have to point out the obvious problem with that if you are a human, and sometimes she 'groomed' between my thumb and first finger – and it hurt, but I couldn't be cross with her. When it was my turn to carry on with cheek rubs and nose strokes, I was unceremoniously reminded by having my hand butted by her head and putting her head under my hand.

Normally she stayed hunkered down for loves but more recently she stretched out more and if flumped[25] down on her side beside the pillow, we would both fall asleep with my arm stroking her side.

Mabel ready for cuddles with mum.

---

[25] A flump – as I called it – is where a bunny doesn't just lie on its side gently, but rather throws itself onto its side with considerable gusto, indeed Missy bless her used to do it with such enthusiasm she would sometimes go all the way over onto her back!

She loved her face being stroked with finger and thumb up her nose and down her cheeks or vice versa in a circular motion. She would sit having this done for hours and hours and if I stopped she would lift her head as if to ask 'why'? Sometimes I got an appreciative chunner doing this but most chunnering was done when she was being kissed on the top of her head. On each occasion, she would reach forward to touch noses first[26], and the fact that she would then bury her head into my open hand so I could give her a complete cheek rub showed a complete trust as her eyes were completely closed and covered.

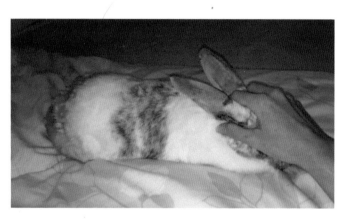

Mabel enjoying a very trustful head massage

---

[26] An additional aspect to the trust seemed to be her permission to stroke and fuss her on most parts of her body. Many rabbits hate having their noses touched, and their tummy, feet and hind quarters/tails are generally off limits but she was generally relaxed at being fussed wherever over time.

I used to think I was being used as a proxy washcloth as my hand would get licked very enthusiastically then she thrust her head into my hand where she just licked especially if she had slightly weepy eyes[27]; however after several years of this I'm fairly confident there was mutual grooming too as it often seemed to be quite unplanned and more just rapturous pleasure.

At the end of the session, as decided by Mabel, I used to get two quick licks as if to say 'thanks mum that's enough for now' then she would hop off and often give her ears and face a good wash which is the other reason I don't think it was just 100% about her; it was a two-way thing.

She seemingly also didn't understand that mum only has one opposable digit; I frequently had her head thrust between my first finger and thumb for massaging her face, but after a licking frenzy she would then shove her head between my index and ring fingers for more massage. It's a bit like shoving a furry tennis ball between those fingers and it hurts and even hypermobile joints don't compensate.

Interestingly, bunnies seem to almost relish their fur being stroked the wrong way, I suspect it may have

---

[27] Might I suggest this was evidence of basic tool use? Even on her last days, she would lick my hand in just the right place to then thrust her head through so the licked areas wiped her eyes because they were weepy and she couldn't scratch them herself with her back legs or wash with her front paws because she simply couldn't balance.

something to do with their social nature and mutual grooming. What she hated, was being brushed. At night, during stroking, I would surreptitiously pluck tufts of loose fur out of her coat which was the only way I could remove the vast amount of fur she moulted regularly. She had two major moults (spring and autumn) but flying fur was a constant feature. I was permitted to remove loose fur from her face but the rest of her body was off limits. If she was really tufty (and looking a terrible mess) I had to pick her up and hold her while giving her a brush just to avoid her ingesting too much fur herself by grooming. Above all, she hated the fine combs that have become popular, it just pulled at her skin and risked ripping it.

I will admit the vacuum cleaner took a bit of a hammering at these times and on redecoration of my house I was horrified to see how much fur was lodged behind radiator covers that I hadn't been able to remove[28]. I sent some of her clean fur off to a lady who spins and knits pet fur and asked if she could make a toy rabbit; I warned her the bunny fur was fine and flyaway and she said she was used to fine fur. When we next spoke, she agreed my warning that it would end up in her eyes, up her nose, in her ears and mouth etc. was a valid description.

---

[28] I later discovered with the help of my decorator that it pretty much came down to brute force to take them off!

Mabel with the toy rabbit made from her moulted fur.

Bunnies can sweat but unlike other animals, they tend not to. I assume to reduce smell that predators can pick up – but something many owners don't realise till it's too late in hot weather, so her fur was deliciously soft, clean and smelled divine. If I needed a bunny fix, I loved to bury my face in the back of her neck, tell her I loved her and breathe deeply. That last bit had to be done gently as the draught wasn't appreciated, but I usually got an approving chunner.

So back to night-time if, rather than cuddles, it was food she was after and I had read the message wrong, she rejected being fussed by ducking down and folding her ears down and out of the way and hopping away. One of her quirks was that if I stroked her left cheek, her left ear flopped down; it didn't happen the other side. Over time she became less and less tolerant of having her ears played with. While Missy would go into ecstasy having her ears rubbed and moved around, Mabel couldn't bear it as she got older, I suspect because she couldn't balance to give them a good scratch if they tickled.

At night, she had to learn to take note of my sleep movement; she sort of extracted herself from under my hand as she felt it getting heavy and twitching as I fell asleep. Bless her heart, I once had a dream that I was trying to hold onto a large piece of white fabric that had become caught on something and the more it pulled away, the stronger I gripped it. Thankfully I didn't hurt Mabel as that piece of fabric in my hand in my dream, was poor old Mabel. Interestingly she didn't become generally wary of me after that and I can only assume she realised it was done unintentionally.

Her behaviour varied over the years and in the early days, she would jump on me in bed to demand food, most often around 7AM and scrabble at my duvet. If not pacified with some head strokes and fusses, I would get a couple of licks on my hand as a hint that her food was called for. A couple of excited grunts ensued while I reached for and dispensed the pellet food I kept in a container in my bedside drawer. She did at one point get into jumping on my head which wasn't pleasant – a rabbit's back foot in your ear will wake you up! Unbelievably, she even learned to turn on the bedside touch switched light and I had to remove the bulb as she realised turning the light on in the middle of the night was a good way of waking me and getting food. Other strategies have included jumping on my feet and scrabbling at the duvet.

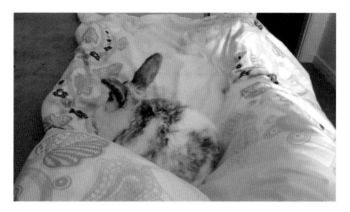

My side of the bed was always more fun

As she got older she just ate what was on the bed, though I did get awoken by the 'hard stare' if I had not (in her opinion) left enough out for her. I cannot explain how this process worked, but as parents of small children know, when you are so attuned to another being, this applies even in your sleep. Waking up aware of beady little eyes boring into your back because you're not giving her loves when she expected them was quite a common occurrence, such that I just got used to lying on my left side so I could give her loves as and when requested.

Earlier in our friendship she used to move away after cuddles and have a darn good wash or simply lie down. In later years she laid down as close to me as she could. In the past she threw herself (flumped) on her side with such energy she threw herself off the bed, so I had to put a chair and barrier up to prevent what could be dangerous falls off a high bed.

Throughout the night she was very much on guard. The slightest noise outside would result in a thumping of the back feet. Any night-time deliveries such as the milkman, or early morning waste collection lorries were greeted by the same ears forward and *thump*! Bunnies don't thump like Disney's Thumper. They lift both back feet off the ground and bring them back down hard, but one foot seems to do more of a thump. I would love to see it in slow motion to see what actually happens. In these situations the only way I could pacify her, was to get up and look out of all the windows and tell her all was well.

Over time, the trust between us developed such that she would be placated by my reassurances and settle back down to being loved. For a while, some of the night she would lie in the hall at the point where she could see all the doorways and later come back up on the bed.

We had a fairly regular routine too regarding getting up in the morning. At around 6AM, she would hop off the bed and go for a snooze. Seemingly this was a very one-way relationship in that I would be kept up all night to love and stroke her, but during the day, she slept. Once we were both 'up' (it's all relative), she would then settle down under the hall seat or on her mat by the conservatory doors, feet firmly tucked under her dewlap[29]

---

[29] The dewlap is a large fold of skin slightly below a bunny's neck that seems to be a fat store, paw coverer, in-situ pillow and a source of downy fur for female buns to make nests with. It will often get stained orange with carrot munching, or pink if cherries have been on the menu.

and fall asleep. I made sure the radio was always on low to keep a level of background noise thereby making any outside extraneous noises less startling.

It became quite clear that Mabel was not happy unless I was up and about; somehow she knew when I was really unwell and had to stay in bed but only a few such days in succession were permitted. Once, when rather unwell, I slept all of Sunday after Saturday night, but this really wasn't acceptable to Mabel. At around 11PM on the Sunday, Mabel started thumping and grunting in the hall. I got up and she hopped to the door of the kitchen and looked in ears forward. I had to get up, go in, check the doors were locked, then she turned to the living room ears forward, I had to go in, check patio doors were locked then she went into the living room and to her litter tray. Maybe it was my imagination but she seemed to want mum to check out the house to ensure it was secure ready for the night.

If I didn't get up when demanded, every effort was made to irritate me into getting up. Morning tactics included hitting the spring style doorstop in the bedroom so it made a loud twang, or pretending to have a chew at the base of the bed. She knew the former would wake me and the latter irritate me enough to get up (it resounds through the mattress and is unwanted damage). I have the usual Perspex panels beside the divan near the bedside cabinets as that often seemed to be a favourite chew zone (any house/any bed) but the morning time chewing was purely for effect. Making the bed with her on it was quite difficult as she wouldn't move out of the way!

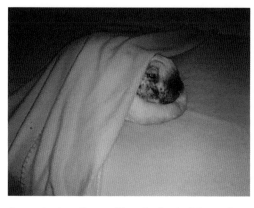

Mabel staying put when I'm making the bed; chin resting on dewlap.

The one time I really got cross with bed chewing, I clapped my hands at her, banished her from the bedroom and she ran away under the kitchen table. I later tried tempting her out with treats but she was not interested and later was very timid. I honestly think she really knew she was in trouble. Another attention seeking option was to jump on the bedside table and skitter scatter across its surface and pretend to have a little nibble at my jewellery box. The one other time I tried to banish her from the bed, I heard her coming in and checking to see if the ramp was in place and when she found it wasn't she came round to my side of the bed which she generally never did, rattled then chomped a temporarily placed cable. When I told her off she then sat in the hall watching me and then even when I went to the loo she turned around and sat and watched me – worse than having small children.

Once she was settled for the day, that was it. The only response one might get during this time was if I made any noise resembling cellophane wrapping being opened. She was acutely attuned to the sound of both the cellophane and her treat box being opened. In either case she would wake up and start circling around my feet again. When she did this, it was very hard to make sure I didn't kick her inadvertently as I walked as she was seemingly fearless. I did accidentally give her a bit of a foot in the ribs when she silently ran up behind me then dashed across in front of my feet. Thankfully because I knew this was a risk, I walked very gently and carefully, went barefoot or with slippers so no harm ever came to her.

Interestingly it seems to be the male bunny preserve (Bertie, LittleMan, and a babysat boy bunny) to go behind you and nip you on the bottom if you are within reach but not showing them enough affection – maybe the human equivalent is a sulk because you've not told them 100 times how marvellous they are for taking the rubbish out!

Mabel also conditioned me, let's face it, it was that way round, that if I had some food e.g. dinner on my lap in front of the TV, she had to be given something to eat too. She would stretch up on her back feet where she easily reached my knee, leaning on me or the chair with her front paws, whiskers twitching like crazy.

She did take a bit of a liking to the biscuits I sometimes got up and ate in the night if my tummy had objected to the cocktail of medicines I took. Even if I ate them in the kitchen, on my return to bed, I was pounced on, sniffed, fingers checked for remnants and so on. I did foolishly give in on occasion and set a bad precedent. I forgot to admit that at the special vets when we were going through her general husbandry. Sometimes when I did give in and take the risk, there might be an unpleasant outcome (upset tummy) if she had anything too human (too much sugar and salt) but sometimes it was just too pitiful to resist. As she got older, I learned to resist as the outcome as it were, can be pretty miserable for both of us, but I did find a human treat we both loved but didn't upset her tummy – seeded oatcakes.

Sometimes at night I was awoken by a significant pooy pong where she has either passed wind or the above has happened (upset tummy). For her sake to avoid fly strike[30] and embarrassment and my sake to ensure hygienic environment she would potentially have to get a midnight bottom wash which normally meant me changing my pyjamas too as they ended up sodden.

She got deeply offended when I tried to sort out her messy bottom by trying to hold her still on the floor long enough to wipe the offending material such as hay or straw away rather than picking her up. However this was met with significant displeasure and was greeted by a thump as she ran to hide under the kitchen table. After that, I just had to pick her up if she needed a clean up.

---

[30] See the Health and Wellbeing chapter for more information about bunny washing and the risk of Flystrike.

It's amazing how much one adapts to life with a bunny without really noticing. I knew not to sit or kneel on the chair she used to jump up on the bed, in the same way I knew not to leave any tantalising cords, belts, scarves dangling from the hall seat etc.. Rather amusingly when my then boyfriend went to use my phone charger in my bedroom, he mistakenly knelt on her chair wearing black cords; simple equation involved there: (White furry rabbit) = (white chair covered in white rabbit fur) ≠ (an ideal fashion accessory to black cords) = (rather grumpy friend).

Interestingly she also learned that mum understood and responded to non-verbal sounds in other instances. Most amazingly once she was tippity tappity claws in the utility room and staying out there, running back to me then back to the utility room. I eventually got up to see what she was up to, and she was sitting upright looking at me, then ran back into utility room. I followed her direction and to my surprise found one of the shrimps from my fish tank in the kitchen had crawled or jumped out of the tank and was in the utility room. I have since discovered that the shrimps are not bred in captivity as it is not possible to replicate their migration and life-cycle. As they have legs and can crawl it's hardly surprising they try to migrate to the salt water where they breed. In the event all three of my shrimp climbed out of the tiny gap in the tank corner and the one live shrimp Mabel found for me only survived a few weeks before trying to migrate again and ended up under my armchair in the living room. I gave up having a fish tank but I firmly believe she wanted to show me that shrimp on the floor, maybe she realised it was in distress, tiny creature though it was.

Obviously because of our strong bond, generally if I needed to travel, she just had to come too, and I travelled with Mabel several times. When she couldn't come with me she stayed with my friend who I trusted her with and reported that while staying there she was far from backward in coming forward. I took that as a good sign that she was a confident rabbit and that she was aware that this was just a visit and that I, her mum, would be coming back to collect her and take her home.

But when with me in a strange place, I set up a large pen with waterproof carpet underneath and all her usual bits and pieces. We have stayed (with permission) in rented cottages, B&Bs, hotel rooms and friends' houses and she never disgraced herself.

On each occasion, we seemed to have an understanding. Although I tried to bunny proof any new place and keep her in a temporary enclosed area unless supervised, she generally didn't play me up too much and would go back into her pen when asked. The command 'bed bed' usually helped convey the message. She was always very good about using her litter tray but her wild instinct to use her dry droppings as territory markers around her litter tray was generally too much to resist, hence the waterproof carpet. It's well known that household cleaning products containing ammonia will make territory marking far worse, a simple steamer or solution of washing soda does the job just as well but with no side effects, and I used this to clean her travel carpet too.

She became very used to travel and albeit reluctantly seemed to understand 'vetty vet vet', as she used to run to her tray for a pee, came back out, try to hide a bit then eventually once in the hall she would eventually hop into her pet carrier. One case in point, she got halfway in then thumped both back feet on the carpet before finally conceding to a gentle push on her bottom to get into the pet carrier properly. Although she was a big bunny, she preferred a smaller carrier than you'd expect as is the case it seems with many bunnies. Maybe it feels more like a burrow that way.

When someone popped their head around the bedroom door to say hello to her and she hadn't realised they were in the house she would sit straight up look squarely at the person raise her chin and almost mouth something to me. I noticed that sometimes we seemed to have a sort of conversation where she would again be sitting very upright, ears up, and as I talked to her, in the conversational gaps or in response to a question, she would move her bottom jaw gently as though she was trying to talk to me or maybe mirror my facial movement and expression.

Mabel chatting

The fact we were so attuned was commented upon by one guest who noticed that while she was supposedly asleep, as soon as she heard my voice an ear would twitch, no matter how quietly I spoke; I hope this was a good sign, I don't think it was because she was scared of me. If you have never watched a bunny fast asleep you have missed a treat. They can sleep with their eyes open but I knew when she was fast asleep as the whiskers twitched, upper lip, eyebrows, ears and mouth twitched and even her body rocked side to side in a deliberate 'cornering' type motion almost if she was running. What do bunnies dream?

The number of expressions and amount of communications that mere eye shape can infer was tremendous. Big wide eyes when excited, softened when acknowledging she was being talked to. She was also able to show a look of absolute disgust if, for example, having gone outside her feet were wet from the grass, they would get flicked dry and I would get a look as if to say it was all my fault.

A very relaxed rabbit.

So that was our 'usual' routine, mum very much manipulated into doing what a certain little bunny wanted but how could I complain? The other key area of her domain was the garden, and it's the management of her safety in this environment that I will cover next.

Chapter 4 – Going Outside (Exploring Like A Rabbit)

The first thing I want to say about taking bunnies outside, is that I wholly disagree with putting a rabbit on a lead. A cat wouldn't be expected to be on a lead and while a dog will get used to it, a rabbit, as a prey animal cannot be expected to tolerate it. I am sure there are many people who have 'succeeded' in acclimatising their rabbit to a harness and lead but I think its fundamentally alien to their world view. They do not like being contained in a harness as this must be akin to being held in a trap or predator's jaws. Then being unable to go in the direction they wish, when one of their escape strategies is to run very fast and rapidly change direction to outwit the predator. Trying to push or pull a rabbit in any direction is generally met with at best disdain and at worst terror.

I will get off my soap box now, though I regret that because of my physical health, I was never able to let Missy and Bertie run in the garden; carrying them up and down stairs from their room (my home office) to the garden was just impossible, and trying to get both back into the house would have been impractical.

With Mabel set up downstairs, she could access outside, though in both houses' gardens I prepared carefully where she would be allowed to run. I didn't want to enclose her in a 'run' as part of their joy at being outside is to run full tilt as long a distance as possible.

Therefore rather like the house, the garden had to be bunny proofed. Though in this case the emphasis was far more on what harm could befall her, than what damage she could do to the garden.

Heather was a favourite.

First was the boundary to be considered. In both gardens, there was secure fencing all the way round, and chicken wire at the bottom of the side gates in case she could squeeze through. In my second garden, I also buried chicken wire under the lawn up to a safe level of the fence which faced out onto open fields; this was as much about preventing a fox or dog from tunnelling underneath as Mabel digging her way out.

In addition to fencing, another safety aspect was the plants included in her area of access. As with houseplants, many garden plants (especially those grown from tubers or bulbs) are poisonous[31]. Thus both gardens at my previous and later addresses, were laid to lawn. The one bush in the second garden that did have mild toxicity she was drawn to like a magnet and would not be deterred from; it was I think a sort of game, as she would only sit beneath it and munch away at the leaves when I was obviously watching her – bunnies are very stubborn! It was also a favourite trick to nibble the point of the rose buds of a very special rose bush I had found on-line, having sought it for 20 years; it was the same variety of rose I had in my wedding bouquet.

Thus the few bushes I did have in situ were checked for toxicity and also kept tidy to ensure no cats or foxes could be hidden from her or me when she went outside. I did nearly have a very nasty incident where unknown to me a cat had secreted itself over the fence and under a bush; when I saw Mabel cowering in the middle of the lawn, then suddenly make a run for it I was horrified to see a cat chasing her. She really was nervous about going out after that and I was amazed the cat would try and attack an animal nearly the same size as it.

The other potential threat to a bunny is any form of carnivorous birds. Crows and Magpies will peck the

---

[31] Rabbits cannot vomit; this may seem to be a bonus for the owner (as recently highlighted on an internet site) but it puts rabbits at serious risk of poisoning; hence it is totally down to the owner to protect them, albeit sometimes from themselves.

eyes of new-born lambs, so I didn't think they would hesitate to have a go at a bunny. We also had several species of raptor in the areas of both the houses that we lived in, who I am sure would regret trying to grab her, but I didn't want the injury and stress of them trying. Thus while keeping hiding places for cats to a minimum, I had to ensure she had hiding places from the skies.

The one final threat to her was other people. While the builders were still working at our second house, they left the front door open. Bunnies are brave little souls and despite everything are very inquisitive, so no surprise that she ran out of the house into the road. Thankfully, it was a quiet road as she had no traffic sense! I think she was too scared and decided to bolt back to the house but she was of course microchipped should she have ever got lost. I've also had trespassers at the bottom of my garden who gave her a terrible fright simply because she never expected to see other humans there.

Mabel would make it quite clear when she fancied going outside in the garden. She either sat at the conservatory doors gazing out onto the patio or pattered back and forth on the vinyl in the kitchen to make the point at the back door. If the back door was opened while she was elsewhere, she could smell the change in air and come running out to investigate.

Once out, she preferred both the conservatory and kitchen doors to be opened and most importantly free from 'things' in her way such as Mum's gardening shoes; these got unceremoniously picked up in her teeth and chucked to one side out of the way. In all fairness, if I needed to be sure of a quick escape to safety I would probably clear the way first too. I'm unsure if it was her eyesight or what, but on one occasion I was standing in the way and she bit me on my foot and was surprised when I yelped. I honestly think she thought it was just another shoe in her way! But it seems to be a bunny thing that they do rehearse where to run to for safety and she used to repeatedly come back to check an escape route indoors and that mum was still available.

Once in the garden, even as an elderly rabbit (aged 10+), she had several mad dashes around the garden, with, if particularly happy with life, some mid-air handbrake turns, jumps of sheer joy known as binkies[32] in the rabbit world. They are the best way to describe these mad leaps in the air with a change in direction at the top of the leap often with a headshake of pure joy thrown in. It is a delight to witness and the sheer joy involved was another lesson learned from Mabel.

Come rain or shine, summer or winter, snow or sunshine (she loved playing in the snow), I sat outside with her.

---

[32] Binkies is the term most rabbit owners use to refer to the jump of joy a bunny will do, often turning their bodies mid leap and a shake of the head. It's a delight to see.

Snow Games

I have been known to sit outside in the depth of winter muffled up in coats, scarves, hot-water bottles etc. just so I could shut the house doors to keep my central heating in rather than warming the planet[33].

---

[33] Indeed as she had full run of house, in 2017 I brought her litter tray into living room rather than lose heat through the conservatory in winter.

Anyway, whilst I either sat and froze in winter, or got bitten to death by mosquitos in summer, the best time to chomp grass was, as one might expect, at dawn and dusk. Therefore they were the times she was happiest outside, though of course the most risky from predators. But the overall purpose of going outside was to eat grass (which is what they should eat always in an ideal world) and enjoy the fun of outside noises, smells and a chance to chase wood-pigeons. She would love to wash her face using rain wetted front paws which were given a vigorous flick to get any dirt off before washing.

Bunnies can flick their front and back legs very effectively and this can be a blessing but also a curse if for example she had managed to pee on the floor where the litter tray usually stood, whilst it was being cleaned. Generally on such occasions she metaphorically kept her legs crossed and waited for her tray to be replaced but if she stepped in any liquid, it would be flicked off. I suspect this is a means of scent marking too if another rabbit is detected. A good hearty pee on a hard floor can be stomped in then flicked up walls, across floors, over skirting boards, up utility room cabinets even as far up as the windowsill – yes, even that far. It's a misplaced scent marking process which especially male unneutered rabbits will do, including to their female, just to be sure she knows as well as everyone else that she belongs to somebunny. Thankfully Mabel never did this to me.

I used to try to let her stay outside as long as possible and if she had had her way she would have been out all night or at least till nightfall. But by that time I couldn't see her well enough to be safe or indeed to get her indoors. Thankfully again, it took only a little time for Mabel to realise that 'bed bed' meant 'I need you to go inside now please'. She often did come in on her own, if startled by something like a blackbird alarm call, but I frequently had to herd her into the house. She would try (and sometimes succeed in) giving me the run-around, but generally she knew mum meant business.

Once indoors I tried to leave it a few minutes so the two actions didn't become continuous cause-and-effect, but I did have to pick her up using the method described above for a bottom check. If the grass was very wet, or she has had an upset tum, or she simply could not reach/couldn't be bothered to 'recycle[34]' it was a good opportunity to check she was clean.

It never ceased to amaze me that no matter what she did, running on wet grass, having a surreptitious dig in the earth behind the bush we think mum couldn't see through, she was always spotlessly clean; her white fur always bright white probably helped by regular moults.

---

[34] Recycling when it comes to bunnies is my way of politely describing the rather unpleasant biological need to pass their food through their digestive tract twice. They produce a caecotroph (part digested food pellet) which they have to eat, and later is passed as the bunny pellets we are all used to. It's the same issue for many herbivores (who have multiple stomachs or chew the cud) in that grass has very low and inaccessible nutrients so much effort has to go into extracting all that's possible.

Perfect pose next to the quince bush

Playing in the garden

Bunny hide and seek

While seemingly a short chapter, being outside and the chance to explore and exercise is such a fundamental need and source of enrichment, that it warrants discussion. Again, these are my observations and opinions, but I do feel they are upheld in the Animal Welfare Act 2006 which states that those responsible for [any] animals must take positive steps to ensure they care for their animals properly and in particular must provide for the five welfare needs, which are:

- need for a suitable environment

- need for a suitable diet

- need to be able to exhibit normal behaviour patterns

- need to be housed with, or apart, from other animals

- need to be protected from pain, suffering, injury and disease.

These are a very simple but essential guide to how to care for any animal. Bunny health and wellbeing as I understand and have experienced it, is the subject of the following chapter.

Chapter 5 – Health And Well-Being (Feeling Like A Rabbit)

I need to caveat the following pages with the clear statement that this is not a 'how to keep rabbits', 'rabbit husbandry', 'rabbit anatomy, physiology and medicine' section. There are many better versions available. It again is about my observations and the various issues Mabel had and how I personally dealt with them. If there was only one thing I would want anyone reading this section to take away from it, is to remember that first, rabbits hide pain and ill health. As a prey species, if you are seen to be weakest amongst your number, you will be targeted so keeping shtum and being stoical is the bunny way. Second, is that in part due to their very fast metabolism[35], a rabbit who appears slightly under par should be taken to a vet immediately. They can go from seeming to be fine to being dead in what feels like microseconds. There is little or no 'wait and see' to be had as poor Missy suffered.

Although this isn't a 'how to' book, I must mention the importance of getting bunnies vaccinated. Humankind (maybe that should be human unkind) has seen fit to introduce a non-native species to a continent then derive the most cruel and horrible way of trying to reduce their numbers. I refer of course to Myxomatosis

---

[35] Heart rates have been recorded between 150 and 300 beats per minute

(Myxi) and Australia. Myxi inevitably came across to the UK population of wild rabbits inflicting a truly cruel disease on these innocent victims. Since inoculation of pet rabbits and a gradual increased resistance to Myxi in wild rabbits, humans very kindly developed a new strain of Myxi that also has to be vaccinated against. In case this wasn't enough, there is also a viral haemorrhagic disease (VHD) which affects rabbits and requires vaccination. And did I mention there are two versions (VHD 1 and VHD 2) of this one too? Humans are just so nice! So that's 4 vaccinations a year[36] (some combined now) every rabbit should have especially if kept outside. These diseases are carried by ticks and fleas both of which will happily reside on a bunny along with ear mites. Around harvest time, they can also be prone to bright orange mites that attach themselves to the eyelids. There is little that can be done about these, and even products for tick and flea control are generally only licenced for cats and dogs and used 'off licence' on rabbits. I often despair at the irony that the products were probably tested on rabbits in their development then the poor little buggers don't even get the benefit of them once commercially available.

Where was I? Ah yes, in general terms, bunnies will hide pain but you can tell if you know your bunny well enough if their behaviour is subdued, they are off their food, panting heavily, stretched right out on their

---

[36] Rabbits are classed as exotic pets; it is quite usual to spend between £1000 and £2500 a year on average on a single rabbit's total care. With the addition of two conservatories built for her, over the 11 years she was with me, I won't tell which of those averages I spent on her, but she was worth every penny.

side or hunched into a little ball. The one sign I looked for with Mabel, which pre-empted all these other signs, was tooth grinding. It's not the same as a pleasure chunner, it's a really 'nails down a blackboard' crunch of the teeth.

Compared with Missy, Mabel was far less of a worry health-wise with respect to tummy troubles, but she had her moments. A common experience (both buns have done it to me and bunny friends have reported similar experiences) is to stop eating, normally due to pain generally, or gastrointestinal pain with accompanying gurgly tummy.

This has to be acted upon immediately. If Mabel refused even her most favourite things such as fresh mint or thyme I knew I had to do something and quickly. As I gained experience with her, I was able to judge when I should dose her with a combination of painkiller, appetite stimulator and stomach acid suppressant, all of which I kept a supply of in the kitchen, prescribed and dispensed by her vet.

The utility room during a poorly bunny spell!

If I was in any doubt that I could handle the situation I didn't hesitate taking her to her vet. Finding a rabbit savvy vet is critical; training has improved immensely, but rabbits still seem to draw the short straw when it comes to veterinary care. They have I suppose in the past been regarded as 'disposable', only expected to live 3-5 years, but as their care improves so too does their life expectancy. One critical difference is how anesthetics are administered. Many bunnies died on the operating table as they simply stopped breathing the anesthetic gasses. A good rabbit savvy vet will intubate a bunny to ensure breathing is properly regulated. This is a highly skilled procedure as the scale of anatomy is tiny.

Mabel going off to sleep[37]

---

[37] With kind permission of Endell Veterinary Group, Salisbury.

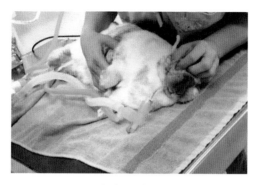

Mabel intubated

A classic example of how a bunny can go off very quickly is as follows; one Friday during the day she was very subdued and by that Friday night she was not much interested in food. By Saturday morning she had apparently not eaten or passed any pee or poo. She was already on antibiotics for a bladder infection and I tried all the usual tricks to get her to eat and medication to help her, but by Sunday morning having been up with her all night, I was now very very worried. She spent all day under the kitchen table which was her 'go to' place if she was feeling threatened or vulnerable. I then started syringe feeding her a fibre rich powder you make up into a paste specifically for such emergencies, as well as more pain killers and the antibiotics. That Sunday she perked up and started eating again and I allowed her to go into the garden. Then there was lots of eating of grass, hopping around and binkies and she wandered along the wall and found my geranium flowers which were apparently very yummy, so too the strawberry plants.

Prized strawberry plants?

Amazingly, even when she was in pain and feeling unwell, she still loved being fussed and I would get appreciative chunnering and licks to say 'thank you'.

It really wasn't uncommon that when we had decided to worry everyone by not eating, needing the medicine every four hours, being checked two hourly overnight wherever she might be in the house (which meant I did spend the odd night on the kitchen floor), without exception the 6PM check would be greeted by bouncing enthusiasm and demands for food, or sitting in the litter tray chomping hay with the look of 'Heck mum, you look awful, have you had a bad night?'.

The only slight difficulty of regular medication is that it has to be orally syringe fed. It's one of the reasons I'm so glad Mabel (and Missy, though initially due to poor handling she scratched me very badly up my arms to the extent my work colleagues thought I was self-harming) allowed me to pick her up and hold her like a baby. Vets seem to manage syringe feeding by holding the rabbits head while holding them on a surface, but either way the secret is to use a 1ml syringe. Regardless of the dose (such that one might have 6 or 7 filled 1ml syringes) the 1ml syringe can be sneaked into the side of the mouth between their front and back teeth even if clenched. With care, if one can get it far enough in so bunny starts trying to chew it, you can also be sure the medicine will get swallowed and not spat/dribbled out. Again though, although Mabel (and in fact most bunnies I've handled) was happy to be held like a baby this was totally different from 'trancing'[38].

For a while, when it was just painkiller I needed to give her and she was eating well, I could often get the medicine into her by soaking a small piece of bread with it. But she soon got wise to this so the bag of chopped bread that was kept in the freezer for just such eventualities, became redundant.

If ever one needed the proof that bunnies hide pain, it was proved in 2015/16; having gone to the vet to investigate a few issues, from x-rays and then a CT scan at a specialist animal clinic in Bath, it transpired she had full-length spondylosis (fusion of the vertebra of the spine through extra bone growth), arthritis in both knees and hips, interstitial pneumonia[39] and the tumour in her reproductive tract.

---

[38] See previous footnote on trancing

[39] Probably from dusty hay earlier in life

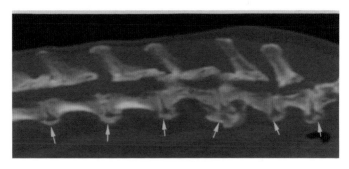

Scan of Mabel's spine: white arrows show extra bone growth between the vertebrae.

Having a sore back did explain why I had noticed that sometimes she was unable to reach round and recycle her caecotrophs and also why she might have been a little overweight. She then weighed in at 3.5 kg. This was fairly standard for her but was apparently too much and in all fairness, she did have a very round tummy and quite a large dew lap. Maybe her usual vet took pity on me regarding the idea of trying to put her on a diet but in some ways I preferred that she had a little excess than was too skinny.

2016: Mabel in the CT Scanner

In February 2019, Mabel started having more problems and seemed to be struggling with a weeping left eye, joined by an itchy sensitive left ear and snuffly laboured breathing; she also started a loud 'gritty' chunnering. Not the 'nails down a blackboard' tooth grinding that she does when in pain, but disturbing nonetheless, especially at night. Over a few days the tooth grinding got to the stage where it was almost constant and she went off her food again. I had to assume after a while that it was low level pain she was experiencing so tried pain killers again; the tooth grinding didn't seem to stop but certainly reduced. Again she was referred to a specialist vet, this time in Swindon for an MRI scan.

I trekked to the specialist practice and delivered a very grumpy bunny. She found travel physically as unpleasant and stressful as I do now, so I don't think I was too popular. Thankfully I had packed an overnight bag in case Mabel had to stay in with the vets till the next day. As I suspected, she had to have a general anaesthetic to deal with some visible tooth issues as well as the MRI scan, and was still barely conscious when I came to see her at 5PM. The vet felt she would be willing to let me take Mabel home as she was, but I was unwilling to risk it; if she failed to pee post op or didn't drink or whatever, plus a long journey, I would be unable to help her, so I left a very dopey Mabel in the care of the vet. A dear friend nearby let me stay with her over-night, and a few glasses of wine helped numb a very sore me and helped reduce my worries about Mabel.

I collected her the next day and came home. The MRI scan was sent to Australia for analysis, and I was given the results over the phone the following day. All I could think was 'The poor little sod'. If ever you need evidence of how well rabbits hide pain this was it. From nose to tail, she had 'something going on' in her right nostril (hence all the sneezing), incisor and molar tooth roots growing the wrong way into her lower jaw. She had interstitial pneumonia diagnosed previously but now had emphysema and a heart murmur to add to that list. She had arthritis in her shoulders and elbows, severe spondylosis (some of which was larger than the vertebra themselves), urinary tract stones, and several other soft tissue problems including the previously diagnosed 'mass' in her abdomen from her spay operation. Her seemingly limited mobility in her back legs (actually more to do with her spine) was what was causing her to pee a bit skewwhiff and causing some staining of her beautiful white fur on her legs. I was devastated. I felt so guilty; was I being selfish keeping her alive?

Around that time she seemed unwilling to eat anything which required significant crunching[40] and I did investigate the idea of having her bottom teeth removed, but yet again she bounced back. From all the diagnosed conditions I assumed she must be in pain and started her on a regime of pain killers[41]. However she soon made it very clear that she really didn't want to be regularly medicated.

Over the next few weeks, Mabel's health deteriorated, and seemingly she was often in pain which was apparently only partly covered by Tramadol etc.. She often lost her appetite and often seemed unable to pee. I knew she had urinary tract stones which must have made things uncomfortable for her. Again, it's part of the lot that mother Nature has deemed to give the rabbit, is an inability to control the amount of calcium they absorb from their diet. Such that they absorb all there is in the food and get rid of the excess in their pee. This obviously is a recipe for kidney, bladder and urinary tract stones.

My vet and others suggested it was maybe time to put her to sleep, but, then again, she would seemingly bounce (almost literally) back. One week she demolished

---

[40] Frankly if my tooth roots were boring their way through my bottom jaw I think I would be reluctant to chew hard food too.

[41] If you have to quarter a tablet not designed to be quartered, as is the case with Gabapentin, it can be an invaluable help to buy some jewelry scales; measuring a ¼ of a tablet as 0.031g made life a lot easier.

her entire weeks' worth of cavolo nero in three days. She finished off five mint and Greek basil growing herb pots and enjoyed the garden again and grass.

Herb heaven

The down side to all these greens? Well a rather gurgley squirty tummy[42], which sent her back into a spiral of pain. I started syringe feeding her with her pellet food made into a very runny paste by soaking the pellets in water (about 30ml) which she had twice a day with her pain killers that I restarted, and she hated me for it. It was a big decision whether to medicate[43] as

---

[42] Perhaps unbelievably, above all, lettuce is not good for bunnies and will send their tummies into all sorts of trouble.

[43] As already stated, they don't show pain so it's very hard to know. Even when she fell off the bed, despite my efforts to prevent it, she was clearly in pain afterwards, but hid under the kitchen table. I suspect one of the pain killers I used once made her very wobbly which must have been very frightening for a bunny who must always feel able to run at a moment's notice.

Mabel always hated being picked up and I daresay now it hurt, as she 'screamed' when being placed back on the floor, however gently. I asked the vet about it, who was of the view that it was yet again a little bit of mummy manipulation because she didn't do the same when the vet did it. What occurred to me more recently was whether she trusted me enough to show pain, but hid it when at the vet, who knows.

Out in the garden again, she even managed a partial mid-air handbrake turn in delight at being outside. When in the hall under the hall seat, she again popped her little head out to see if I had a treat for her, or a head rub. At the sound of cellophane, again she'd come running over in case there was a treat on the cards; could I put her to sleep when she was still getting pleasure from life?

I am absolutely sure in my heart that she was managing any pain because she went almost back to normal, and not just eating, drinking and grooming, but running, jumping and chunnering when stroked and loved.

Anyway, going back to the weeping eyes, that tends to be a big alarm bell for teeth troubles in rabbits. Her left eye wept particularly and she would go bald in that area where the crusted fur came off. I did notice a funny yeasty smell around her eyes and her vet kindly flushed her tear ducts just in case they were blocked and causing the weeping. She had this done several times along with antimicrobial eye drops but it seemed to be an intermittent recurring feature with her; by then she was an 8-year-old rabbit, so I had to expect some issues. As such when her eyes were bad, I sometimes used tepid water and cotton wool pads just to ease the stickiness of the fur under her eyes. She hated it to begin with but once she realised the relief it gave, she seemed to enjoy it, but not for long – I was made well aware when I had overstepped the mark. She tended to scratch at her eyes with her back feet and on one occasion, when she paused, I looked at her and said why don't you wash baby? As I said it, I pretended to lick my hands and rub them cupped over my face like a bunny would wash. She looked at me and then did exactly the same washing her face and her damp fur round her eyes with her front paws. Maybe coincidence but again, who knows.

As far as washing was concerned, I was having to clean her up a fair amount whilst minimising how wet she got, but in August 2019 I had to clean her up as her tail end was a real mess but to my horror, I hurt her. In trying to sort out a bad clump of matted fur I tore the skin underneath. Bunny skin is so fine and fragile you really are at risk of ripping it if you try to pull too hard on any matted fur. Better to trim it, but again you have to be careful as it's very easy to pull up the skin and cut that by mistake. There was no point me taking her to the vet over it, as they would not anaesthetise a rabbit for the sake of putting stitches in such a tiny wound and it healed quickly.

In all the years I had her, she never knowingly hurt me, she never deliberately bit me once in anger and I put that down to our very special relationship and the wonderful trust she had in her mum. But obviously time passes and we all get old and dealing with the issues that arise with an elderly rabbit require another level of understanding again.

CHAPTER 6 – Getting Old (Bunny Style)

What does it take to keep an elderly bunny happy? All the same things as before but with a little more prompting, help and sympathy. Becoming more disabled and in pain myself, I could understand some of what she was going through. I used to just take food/ treats to her wherever she was and made it as fun and various as possible e.g. fresh thyme, carrot tops, mint etc.. It was only much later in her life I discovered that despite rejecting nearly all soft fruit, she liked cherries. I never saw her eat a whole one and wondered how the stones were always so clean if she just bit the fruit off it. Then I saw how she did it, she bit off what she could then sucked the stone clean, spitting it out just as we would.

I tried to get her to put on weight, as I could tell she was getting thinner, so decided to try her with Waitrose muesli – she would take what she wanted then, if I didn't get there quickly enough, she would pick up the pot with her teeth and chuck it (spilling the contents in the process) out of her way.

In later life she hated her ears being tickled or touched and sometimes when I was kissing her head my hair tickled her ears and she got very grumpy with me. But as she got still older (around 2019-20 when she was probably aged 10+) and her balance got worse she was unable to do what I called her ballet dancer pose to keep her legs and feet clean. I was never able to get a photo of her in this pose. I could support her to have a good back-foot ear scratch, the independent earlier version of which is captured in the following photo.

Itchy face? Ooh that's better.

Then when she couldn't balance to wash her ears with her front paws, I was permitted to pull her ears to her mouth so she could lick them and do a single paw wash. Even the 'no go zones' no longer seemed to matter and I could kiss the tops of her feet etc.. One night I woke to find I was stroking one of her back feet which was stuck out in a funny pose; being allowed to touch a foot is unheard of, so I guess the love was more than just one way.

As she got older, around nine years, I noticed she was finding it harder and harder to jump up on the bed. I was also worried about the impact on her joints of jumping down from a high bed, so I placed a chair next to the bed that she could use as a step up and down. It was also a safety measure with her habit of throwing herself on her side (flumping) so vigorously that she fell off the bed. Over the years, looking back at the many photos and videos, I must have tried one hundred and one configurations of her side of the bed to facilitate access, prevent falls or mishaps.

Chair in situ, though we always preferred Mum's side of the bed.

Later in summer 2018, I noticed her back legs were losing power and even the chair was proving a challenge, so I added one, then two inverted plastic storage boxes covered and edged with carpet to ensure she had grip, and they didn't move as she jumped up. I also put a ramp into her litter tray in the living room; anything greater than around 15 cm seemed to be too big a step. Interestingly though, whilst vacuuming I had removed the two boxes but still found her on the bed later; but she was very out of breath and I got a serious disapproving stare.

Bunny steps

But as the photos tell, at the same time she was losing mobility, she started to lose her thus far immaculate litter training and started peeing on the bed. I wondered if maybe she could jump up the boxes in steps but couldn't get down again due to her joint and spinal problems, so in September that year (2018), I created a ramp made with 2.2 m pine board covered in carpet to aid traction. This was after much trial and error, and for a few nights she wouldn't use the ramp, then one day I just found her on the bed. I guess the prospect of cuddles was more important than dealing with '*a new thing*'.

Obviously now I had to stop her from coming onto my side of the bed; I manage to rig up a cardboard divider between us with just enough room at the top for me to get my arm in to love and stroke her, which she still came to bed for every night.

Ramp in the background; cardboard divider foreground.

As a solution to getting on and off the bed quickly enough, the ramp worked for a few months but after a while the peeing got worse again. I realised she was struggling to get to her litter tray in the living room in time, probably due to her urinary tract stones making peeing uncomfortable[44], instead tending to go when and where she could and wherever she was sleeping/resting.

One of the many options I tried really shows there was no greater love this bunny mum had for her bunny, I put a very shallow litter tray on her side of the bed where the pillows should be, surrounded by incontinence pads (inco-pads). It could get pretty whiffy when she pee'd, but the paper and hay seemed to absorb smell, and as long as I cleaned the tray daily, it was manageable.

---

[44] Rabbit pee is notorious for turning bright orange/red due to certain foods such as parsley. However this can mask blood in the urine which is a sign the bunny needs to see a vet asap.

One of the many iterations of sleeping arrangements; litter tray on the bed!

However soon even this wasn't a solution as she just seemed to have to go when she had to go wherever that was. I had already eventually relented and swapped fleece throws for large inco-pads as the fleece throws would become saturated with just plastic under them. I hated the implications of using these on the environment (having to go to landfill) but I had no choice. The benefit of inco-pads was that they wicked away the pee and reduced the amount she got on herself[45]. At one point though she started chewing them and I was worried about the harm the moisture absorbing gel in them could do to her, never mind the papery cover. The compromise

---

[45] The only time I ever had to put her in the bath (in 1 inch of tepid water), was in 2019. While cleaning I had put her in the conservatory on several inco pads which she managed to totally miss, instead peeing on the vinyl flooring; the pee only had one place to go when walked in – all over her dewlap, tummy, four furry feet and tail.

transpired to be very old fleece throws cut up into the size of her area of the bed, allowing pee to drain into the inco-pads to keep her dry, and removing the risk she would chew and ingest the gel.

I ended up with inco-pads covered in fleece throw pieces all over my bed, as well as in the hall, living room and kitchen, basically in all her favourite places to rest or sleep. I reckoned that if I am still alive let alone continent when I am 100, I will be impressed!

With all her mobility issues, in June 2019 my vet suggested physiotherapy and Mabel was referred to a well-regarded practitioner Fiona, who practised in the owners' home. Fiona was so kind and lovely to Mabel and although I suspect she was more used to treating horses, cats and dogs she helped greatly, and it was a little bit of a learning experience for both of us. She successfully gave Mabel laser treatment to her back legs, as Mabel seemed to be unable to weight bear on her left foot; I also noticed that Mabel's tail was leaning left quite a bit, which Fiona manipulated to release the tension to great effect. A lasting memory for me will be Fiona lying on the hall floor as I sent Mabel back and forth so she could see how well and straight Mabel was hopping and both of us ending up in giggles. I'm not sure how many practitioners would have done so much to try and help Mabel and I am forever thankful.

In August 2019, Fiona noticed a deficit in Mabel's front right side and queried a stroke, but these symptoms soon passed. The fact that I was allowed for the first time ever to put my arm completely around Mabel's little bunny body for a cuddle, for which I got some arm licks, made me think perhaps she was feeling vulnerable.

Gradually her range reduced over time, from accessing the whole house, to just the bedroom and then just the bed. I used the bottom of the pet carrier, which she could hop in and out of up until the last, as a tray to put her on and off the bed. By this time I had wire fencing panels around her side of the bed to stop her falling off, though she did manage to tip herself out of the carrier down in between the bed and the fencing, so I had to tighten up the fencing panels and anchor them better.

Her new burrow

I also noticed that her beautiful white tail, back legs and bottom were getting stained yellow because she couldn't 'hover' to pee. So cleanliness became a bit of an issue. She clearly couldn't reach to groom that area anymore (including her scent glands near her bottom that took a nose peg for mum and damp cotton wool buds to sort out). But I noticed her hocks were getting sore, and on one check I noticed they were red raw. As this was during the Covid 19 outbreak, Mabel couldn't actually see the vet but by telephone we arranged I would collect some cotton wool and bandages which initially worked really well. She didn't try chewing at them at all and as a solution it was initially very effective though I was paranoid about not tightening the bandages too tight and cutting off a blood supply to her feet. After a while though, as she became less able to pee straight, the cotton wool got wet and risked the urine burning the skin even more. As a result, I just kept her on veterinary fleece which did the job of relieving the pressure whilst also keeping her dry.

Little bandaged feet.

From February 2020, I noticed she was lying with crossed front legs. I had no idea why, but she seemed to balance better. I was unable to get her to see the physio due to Covid 19, and there were many occasions when she tipped onto her side then struggled to get up. I had to 'right' her and at night I was only lightly asleep, as I would be awoken by the frantic paddling of her back legs trying to get upright. Sadly this happened in April, the last time she went into the garden (with help) where after a lovely sunbathe[46] she fell on her side and couldn't get up. I think she found this terrifying.

---

[46] Bunnies love to sunbathe as long as they are kept cool; the sunlight is also essential for their vitamin D levels so keeping rabbits constant darkness is not good for them physically or psychologically.

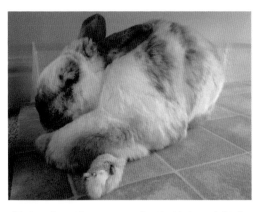

Sitting with her front legs crossed – that's her right front paw!

In spring 2020 she seemed to want to stay in my bedroom, even unwilling to sit under the hall seat, a past favourite location. Then I was just moving her, in her carrier, from the corner of the bedroom to the bed at night and vice versa in the morning. I realised this was probably unnecessary stress and movement so eventually she just stayed on the bed, safe with the fencing around it, the inco pads to keep her clean and the veterinary fleece to protect her feet.

I had always promised her that if she didn't make the decision for me, I would know when the time was right to let her go; well how naïve was I? I reckoned when she stopped objecting to being picked up, grooming herself, eating or stopped thumping her disapproval I would know she was near the end. However, it didn't work out that way.

I spent every moment I could with her, and she came up the bed to me for fusses and cuddles at every opportunity. Every time I had to pick her up, I would kiss her furry feet and thank her for being such a wonderful companion. She continued grooming (even on her last day) by using my hand as a proxy washcloth to clear her eyes. She continued, above all, to chunner her pleasure at being loved, and hopped over when she heard her treat bag rustling.

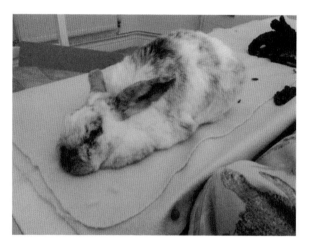

Getting old

And she still made me laugh; while I was cleaning, I had to put her somewhere while I changed the bed and sheets under all her inco-pads and fleece. I put a fleece in the bathroom, so she could sit still and in comfort, but it wasn't disastrous if she pee'd by accident as it was a vinyl floor which I assumed she would avoid walking on as she was already unsteady on her feet. But when I went back into the bathroom to collect her and put her back on the bed, she had obviously had a nose around and managed to collect all the dust and fluff that collects every week behind the bathroom door on her whiskers.

The following Friday she was clearly in pain, with her front legs crossed and back legs splayed to keep her balance, though the tale tell sign of back pain, to walk as opposed to hop, she was still resolutely not showing me. I managed to get regular doses of very strong pain killers into her hidden in her treats. That Saturday, I had to wash her as her bottom fur was saturated with urine as she really couldn't pee properly anymore. I hated getting her fur so wet, but the urine was scalding her skin and her dear little tail was losing its fluffy fur. Normally I was given the cold shoulder after being washed, but when I went into the bedroom to check on her later, she was at my end of the bed wanting fusses so I went to bed and just put my arm around her on the bed and loved and fussed her for hours. That evening I also noticed she was struggling to get to her water bowl and again fell over in the night several times, which I awoke to quickly and 'righted' her. In spite of all this I was given a lot of bunny kisses, (quick licks) as if to say 'I forgive you mum'. I knew she was scared and in pain.

That week, and particularly that night, she ate lots of cherries, mint, thyme, lavender, rose buds etc. but she wasn't really interested in her usual food and seemed unable to hop over for her treats. Over the course of the Saturday, having spoken to the vet and to the pet crematorium, I had decided I needed to let her go on the Monday. So at 8:45AM Monday the 15th June 2020, I rang the vet and they kindly fitted us in before they started their surgical list. They took her from me out of the car because Covid 19 required social distancing, to insert a cannula in her ear without me and obviously sedated her before bringing her back to me. I hadn't realised she would be so sedated, and in my anxiety not to upset her by my distress, I had handed her over to the veterinary nurse without giving her a kiss, saying I loved her or goodbye as I assumed I could do that when she was brought back to me. But she was unconscious when they handed her back to me and that last knowing kiss never happened, and it kills me.

I know they did their best to make a terrible moment as least traumatic as possible by using a long line into her ear, so I could hold her while they injected her (whilst ensuring social distancing), but it meant I saw the anaesthetic that would end her life travelling into her little ear. I so desperately wanted to shout 'Stop, I've made a mistake' but I knew what I had to do. She shuddered as she died which is apparently normal so even though I knew I had to do it, it felt like a total betrayal of her trust in me. By 9:20AM or so she was gone. They took her back to tidy her up and remove the fluid line in her ear and gave her back to me wrapped up in a fleece.

I was, and still am in writing this, beside myself with grief. I came home, took her ear bandage off and cleaned her up (I didn't want to do it before and get her all stressed), so she arrived at Dignity Pet Crematorium[47]

---

[47] Dignity Pet Crematorium. Odiham Road, Winchfield, Hook, Hampshire

with a clean bottom, relatively clean paws and sprigs of lavender, mint and thyme, her favourites. I dropped my darling baby girl off at the pet crematorium at 11:45AM and waited so I could bring her ashes home. They had to weigh her and my poor little girl was only 2kg at the end, she was 3.45kg most of her life.

After everything I had done to keep Mabel alive, I couldn't stop the passage of time. She was my unflinching, uncomplaining, trusting, stoical, delightful, beloved companion for 11 years. She saw me though so much with unconditional love and has left a yawning gap in my life. I cannot begin to describe the pain and loss. Waking up the next morning without an eager bunny on the bed demanding cuddles was a nightmare come true.

Unless you have been there, it's hard to understand the rollercoaster of having a bunny friend with the ups and downs, well-poorly-well-poorly and the chicken and egg dilemma of pain in their gut leading to anorexia leading to pain. With all her other ailments, there was the constant responsibility of possible euthanasia hanging over us, as was suggested several times before.

I knew Mabel had gone, the house felt totally empty, however two very odd things happened. I am not spiritual at all, but I will admit I was a little spooked at the coincidences of life. The following two days I had my music on rather than the radio, and it was set to random shuffle on my IPod; on both occasions, I would start it with my choice of song, then the next track would be 'Bright Eyes' by Art Garfunkel, the theme from the first animated film version of Watership Down. Then the same thing happened in the car on my phone music.

Later that week, on Wednesday night I awoke because I was sure I felt hops on the bed; I know this was just my brain trying to cope/process it all, but all Thursday I felt comforted as though she was with me. That evening I said to her to go wherever she is happiest and come Friday, the house felt empty again. I hope she's gone wherever bunnies go, where there is green pasture, where no-one picks you up and washes your messy bottom and no-one cuts your toenails!

The loss is painful; I never really understood what people meant by heartbroken, but I know now; it physically hurts and I feel sick with grief. But several people have said, stopping their suffering even though you know it will break your heart, is the last greatest act of love you can do for a treasured animal.

Bunny footprints on the bed and in my heart

Epilogue

As I hope has become clear, all rabbits have fabulous characters with their own unique little reactions to what's happening in the world. They are sentient beings, evolved to live in complex social groups which require mutual respect and adherence to social bunny norms of behaviour.

What is really fundamental is not that we need to realise and understand they are sentient beings, they need to realise that *we* are. Also that you can be communicated with and that you will behave, understand their communications and react to them consistently. Sadly, I don't think she was particularly unusual[48], it's our failings that mean these beautiful creatures never get to express their true personalities. Anecdotally I think they choose you. Missy came to me in the pet shop and Mabel chose me at the rescue.

The relationship was so special because she was a prey animal yet trusted me implicitly. She was wholly dependent on me for everything, but still held her head high and let me know if I crossed the acceptability line in cleaning a messy bottom or trying to groom her. The size of her personality and presence far outstripped her physical size.

---

[48] Though the kind messages about her that I received from her vet team, her physio, her rescue and many others when they heard the news, all said she was a special girl and our bond with each other was amazing.

I know I was fortunate to have the time to spend with her and I know it was a very uniquely close relationship we had. This isn't possible for everyone, but I hope that my experiences and observations can be of use to those looking to understand their beloved bunnies better too and show them their potential.

I am not the only rabbit lover who fervently believes that bunnies shouldn't be regarded as a 'first' pet; They take *a lot* of time and money. They are fundamentally inappropriate as 'cuddle pets' as they simply don't like being held especially off the floor. If you need to hold and cuddle an animal get a cat or dog. Rabbits take a long time to trust enough to be able to be held without struggle. It's not rocket science to assume that if a rabbit is struggling (or biting) while being held it must be suffering stress.

Rabbits get ignored; most animal welfare charities that advertise for funds show multiple cats and dogs in need, but no rabbits yet they are one of the most numerous pets in the UK so by default must get the lion's share of abuse. But rabbits don't 'look pathetic'. They are very stoical because they are prey animals. They don't mew or whimper or bark to let you know something is wrong.

When will these fabulous creatures be appreciated? Who knows; I hope maybe this book will go some way to changing opinions, and it was my promise to my beautiful girl that I would write this and try and better the lot of the average pet bunny.

'What more photos mum?'

Printed in Great Britain
by Amazon